COLUMBIA ESSAYS ON MODERN WRITERS

M^W

NUMBER 39   PRICE $1.00

72

WILLIAM EMPSON

by J. H. Willis, Jr.

William Empson

By J. H. WILLIS, Jr.

Columbia University Press

NEW YORK & LONDON 1969

COLUMBIA ESSAYS ON MODERN WRITERS is a series of critical studies of English, Continental, and other writers whose works are of contemporary artistic and intellectual significance.

Editor: William York Tindall

Advisory Editors
Jacques Barzun   W. T. H. Jackson   Joseph A. Mazzeo

William Empson is Number 39 of the series

J. H. WILLIS, JR. is Associate Professor of English at the College of William and Mary.

Copyright © 1969 Columbia University Press
Library of Congress Catalog Card Number: 74–76254
Printed in the United States of America

Acknowledgment is gratefully made to Chatto & Windus, Ltd., for permission to quote extracts from poems in William Empson's *Collected Poems* and extracts from his *Seven Types of Ambiguity* and *The Structure of Complex Words;* to Harcourt, Brace & World, Inc., for permission to quote extracts from poems in *Collected Poems;* and to New Directions for permission to quote extracts from *Seven Types of Ambiguity*, *Some Versions of Pastoral*, *The Structure of Complex Words*, and *Milton's God* (© 1961 by William Empson), all rights reserved.

William Empson

William Empson will be remembered for his *Seven Types of Ambiguity*. With this work of literary criticism, Empson modified the vocabulary of criticism and illustrated a method of close verbal analysis which, while not entirely original, was original in its extensive application and illustrative examples. No one having penetrated beyond the first few pages is likely to forget the astonishing demonstration of Empson analyzing one line from Shakespeare's Sonnet 73 ("Bare ruined choirs, where late the sweet birds sang"). But Empson, the critic, is the author of more than one significant book. He is also a poet worth remembering.

Knowledgeable T. S. Eliot, writing about Dr. Johnson, once emphasized the relevance of studying a critic's poetry or a poet's criticism. From Dante to Johnson, Coleridge, or Arnold, the poet-critic reveals his concerns in both his creative and his critical endeavors, the one illuminating the other. Rarely, however, as with T. S. Eliot, do the two merit equal attention. Empson is not alone in being better known as a critic than as a poet, although he first wrote poetry, and although his poetry was particularly admired in the 1950s by young poet-critics. The peculiar aspect of his literary career is that much of his reputation stems from work which he started as an undergraduate at Magdalene College, Cambridge: *Seven Types of Ambiguity* (1930) and *Poems* (1935).

Empson, himself, started in 1906 at Yokefleet Hall, Howden, Yorkshire, where the Empson estate borders the river Ouse. A Yorkshireman from a long line of Yorkshiremen (he recog-

[3]

nized the regional characteristics by calling Satan a country-man), he is presently a professor of English literature at Sheffield University in North Riding. Between beginnings and present, however, Empson's circuit of travels has taken him far from the northern counties. After Cambridge, Empson taught English at the Bunrika Daigaku University, Tokyo, from 1931 to 1934. Back in England, he spent a few productive years writing articles and reviews, and publishing two books, before returning to the Orient in 1937. He joined the English faculty of the Peking National University in China just as the Sino-Japanese war erupted. For two perilous, uncomfortable years he followed the exiled and refugee universities from Peking to Yunnan Province, teaching the metaphysical poets from memory, books being scarce, and writing his own, sometimes metaphysical, poems. During the war years in London, Empson put his Eastern expertise to good use working as Chinese editor for the B.B.C. His efforts at propaganda brought him dubious recognition from the Nazi propagandist Hans Fritzsche who called him a "curly-headed Jew." Neither one nor the other, Empson rather enjoyed this proof of his effectiveness at "argufying." In China once more, after the war, Empson taught English in Peking from 1947 to 1952 during increasingly unsettled years. Twice in this period he flew to Gambier, Ohio, to teach in the Kenyon College Summer School. As a poet subsidized by the British Council, he was partially dependent on English funds. When the Council closed its activities in China, Sinophile Empson, his wife, and his two children returned to England for reasons partly economic, and partly familial. The children, he says, needed educating at home. At home he has remained since joining the faculty of Sheffield in 1953.

Since the impressive and startling beginning of *Seven Types of Ambiguity* published the year after he went down from the University, Empson has produced three more influential and

[4]

controversial books of criticism: *Some Versions of Pastoral* (1935), *The Structure of Complex Words* (1951), and *Milton's God* (1961). In addition he has been a prolific writer of articles and reviews, so that, continuing to grow, the canon of his criticism bulks large. The reaction to Empson's criticism has usually been spirited, often heated, alternately pleasing or annoying serious readers of literature, while he, in turn, has pursued his critics in lively rebuttals. Whatever view of his criticism is adopted, the work is never ignored, and not easily forgotten. It remains constantly near center stage, praised or blamed by an alert audience.

Empson's poetry, in contrast, has remained in the wings, or, at best, somewhere on the fringes of the central action. Unlike his critical writing, Empson's composition of poetry has never been extensive. He has produced only two slim volumes, *Poems* (1935) and *The Gathering Storm* (1940), which were later combined to form the *Collected Poems* in two editions (1949, 1955). With few exceptions, Empson's fifty-five collected poems were written either in the late 1920s, while he was an undergraduate, or during the next decade. Although, as he himself admits, he may write poetry again, his reputation as a poet now rests on a body of work largely completed by 1940.

The origin of both *Seven Types* and *Poems* is particularly Cantabrigian. Empson, who studied mathematics, earning a "First" in the subject, changed in his third year to the study of English, winning a starred "First" on the English Tripos under the tutelage of I. A. Richards. In addition to his academic achievements, Empson's contribution to the intellectual life of Cambridge was considerable and varied. He wrote and directed a rather Freudian play, *Three Stories*. He published an impressive amount of poetry and criticism, and in his capacity of literary editor or reviewer he contributed articles, book reviews, and movie reviews to the *Cambridge Review* and to *Granta*, the prestigious university magazines. Perhaps more significantly, Empson was a co-founder and co-editor of *Experiment* in 1928, a highly successful and controversial undergraduate magazine which seems to have lived up to its name. His abilities in mathematics, science, and literature made him a man of the hour at a time and place which was significantly interdisciplinary in attitude. Cambridge, during the 1920s when Empson was a student, was the center of important developments in the physical and natural sciences, particularly physics and astronomy, in philosophy, linguistics, history, and literature. The students as well as the dons excelled in often extremely diverse fields. C. P. Snow, later novelist and formulator of the two-cultures controversy, was busy in the Cavendish Laboratories earning a Ph.D. in physics in 1929 when, as he should have realized, the cultures at Cambridge were remarkably unified.

No wonder, then, that Empson in his poetry and criticism should reflect the current interests in science, philosophy, and psychology. If Sir Arthur Eddington's popularizing books on the new science were influential to the scientifically minded literati, so too were the writings of T. S. Eliot, Robert Graves, and I. A. Richards. Although Empson never says so, Eliot can probably be credited with influencing the critical methods Empson developed. In such early essays as "Tradition and the Individual Talent" (1919), "The Perfect Critic" (1920), "Imperfect Critics" (1920), and "The Function of Criticism" (1923), Eliot affirms the importance of an impersonal, analytical, critical intelligence operating on a literary text to present the reader both with external facts and with evaluations based on the work of art as an autonomous whole. "Comparison and analysis," says Eliot, "are the chief tools of the critic." Empson, however, does acknowledge the work of Robert Graves and Laura Riding as contributing to his technique of verbal analysis. Calling Graves the inventor of the method, in

[6]

his preface to the second edition of *Seven Types*, Empson has in mind the Graves and Riding book *A Survey of Modernist Poetry* (1927) wherein they read closely and attend to syntax, spelling, punctuation, and alternative meanings of words. Neither their approach, however, nor Graves's earlier writings on the importance of the underlying associations of each word in a poem is systematic. They merely suggest, occasionally, what Empson will make into a full-scale *modus operandi.*

It is to Richards, more than to any other, that Empson feels indebted, often stating in the prefaces and texts of his criticism his adaptation of ideas derivable from his mentor. Combining psychology and semantics, the writings of Richards (especially *Principles of Literary Criticism, Science and Poetry*, and *Practical Criticism*—all written in the 1920s) emphasize the logical, analytical, nearly "scientific" approach to literature. Poetry, says Richards, is a "limited piece of experience" which is "communicable." As he stresses analysis, communication, and careful attention to literary texts, Richards points the way Empson will follow. He may even have suggested to Empson the use of "ambiguity" as a critical term, for in *Science and Poetry* Richards stated that most words in poetry are ambiguous. It is up to the reader, he said, to choose the meaning most satisfying the impulses stirred by the form of the poem.

Empson learned much from Richards, and followed at least some of his teacher's suggestions when writing *Seven Types*. The genesis of the book is amusingly recounted by Richards who described his role as Empson's Director of Studies for the English Tripos. After Empson, to the astonishment of Richards, had played some games of interpretation with Shakespearean sonnets, he commented to Richards that he thought it could be done with any poetry. Richards, with relief, sent him off to do it. Empson returned three weeks later with the central portion of what would become *Seven Types of Ambiguity*. He seems

[7]

to have discovered and perfected his critical approach to literature in one step. No matter how much he subsequently modified the first draft, nor how much he developed independently of Richards, his technique of verbal analysis, so consistently used throughout his critical practice, is clearly inaugurated in this book.

Seven Types of Ambiguity is a remarkable work, none the less so because it is so obviously a young man's book. Its excesses or insufficiencies are those of a young man, although a particularly brilliant one. The argumentative edge and jaunty tone, the appeal to common sense in uncommon judgments, the disarming admission of inconsistencies, the inaccuracies, the eclecticism of supporting evidence, and the uneven prose style all give the book its particular quality of youthfulness and zest. It is clearly a thesis book presented with boldness, reflecting the varied, but spotty, reading of an unusually perceptive student. Empson smoothes off some of the rough spots in style and argument in his second edition, but the book in any edition stands as a unique achievement.

Empson's title, challenging belief in the magic number of his types, is characteristic. Why not three, or five, or even nine, one might ask? In 1926 T. E. Lawrence, probably remembering Ruskin, had published his discovery of Wisdom's seven pillars, and wise Empson may have enjoyed suggesting Lawrence's title. But, in fact, there might be almost any number of types. In his preface to the second edition, Empson says that he uses the term "ambiguity" to mean anything he likes, and comments that the distinctions among the seven types "would not be worth the attention of a profounder thinker." Laer in the book he admits that type three (the pun) is related to the fourth, that the sixth may be included in the fourth, that the fourth may belong in either the fifth or sixth, that the sixth may fall in the seventh, and vice versa. Near the end of *Seven Types* he candidly admits

[8]

that the types may appear trivial or indistinguishable one from another, but that they "form an immediately useful set of distinctions" which may heighten one's consciousness of the cases themselves. Empson is concerned not with classifying ambiguities but with applying his method of verbal analysis to a wide variety of literary texts, substantiating his belief that the logical examination of poetic language leads to understanding and greater appreciation of the beauties of verse.

An ambiguity, as he defines it in the beginning, is "any verbal nuance, however slight, which gives room for alternative reactions to the same piece of language." He arranges the seven types of these ambiguities, each discussed in a separate chapter, in "stages of advancing logical disorder." The arrangement, if nothing more, provides structure for what would otherwise be a loose collection of illustrative examples. The seven disordered types range in complexity from the first, when "a word or a grammatical structure is effective in several ways at once," to the seventh, when "the two meanings of the word . . . are the two opposite meanings refined by the context, so that the total effect is to show a fundamental division in the writer's mind."

Empson's examples, illustrating these types, are the meat of the book, and perhaps the sauce as well. Drawing heavily upon poetry and drama, he subjects passages from thirty-nine poets, five dramatists, and five prose writers to varying degrees of close reading. In spite of the apparent range of the selections, there are some revealing omissions. Empson never mentions Anglo-Saxon literature, and uses only the *Troilus and Criseyde* of Chaucer, briefly, to illustrate types two and six. The sixteenth and the early part of the seventeenth century provide Empson with most of his examples. The writings of T. S. Eliot on Shakespeare and the metaphysicals seem particularly influential here. The post-Restoration period and the eighteenth century, however, are virtually neglected. Milton, for example, is scarcely

[9]

mentioned at all, although Pope is used briefly to illustrate all seven types except the fifth. The nineteenth century, surprisingly, provides a considerable number of examples. The major Romantic and Victorian poets are mentioned, with the interesting omission of Arnold and the extremely brief reference to "Lady of Shalott" under type six. It is the only poem of Tennyson's used in the book. Hopkins's poetry is considered twice— "Spring and Fall" under type four, and a particularly telling examination of "Windhover" under type seven, the most ambiguous of all. Twentieth-century poets receive short shrift, only T. S. Eliot (an excerpt from "A Game of Chess") and W. B. Yeats ("Who Goes with Fergus?") providing important examples for types two and six respectively.

Shakespeare and the metaphysicals are clearly emphasized in *Seven Types*. After his opening analysis of one line from Shakespeare's Sonnet 73, Empson, in the course of the volume, quotes portions of eleven more sonnets, using them to illustrate ambiguities of the second and fourth type. Sonnet 83 receives an especially careful reading. Passages from twelve plays are analyzed, but particularly from *Macbeth, Hamlet, Othello*, and *Measure for Measure*. Not surprisingly, Shakespeare helps illustrate all seven ambiguous types. Among the metaphysicals, Empson utilizes passages from Donne, Marvell, Crashaw, Herbert, and Vaughan, emphasizing Donne's "Valediction of Weeping" (fourth type) and Herbert's "The Sacrifice" (seventh type). Throughout the book, Empson shows himself extremely interested in the metaphysical conceit, its development, witty use of multiple meanings, increasing vagueness in Marvell's poetry, and eventual disintegration into the "jam" of Carew and the "suggestions of conceits" in Vaughan. The importance of this interest in the conceit will be manifest everywhere in Empson's early poetry.

With a few notable exceptions, therefore, Empson is satisfied in *Seven Types* with presenting and developing his method of verbal analysis, limiting its applications to a number of brief selections from the broad spectrum of English literature. No poem or passage is treated thematically or exhaustively in the book, and often a few lines from a poem suffice to illustrate a particular point. His usual method, regardless of length, is to read closely with the N.E.D. in hand, presenting the reader with a series of alternative denotations of an important word. From such brief compendiums, Empson characteristically moves dexterously through related connotations to a frequently original and sometimes startling interpretation of a line. Unworried by sins of Intentional or Affective Fallacies, he freely determines the poet's conscious and unconscious motives, as well as the reader's reactions. Psychology, semantics, and rhetoric combine impressively to yield analyses which seem objective, yet are strangely subjective.

Reading Hopkins's "Windhover," for example, Empson sees the Jesuit poet-priest contrasting the physical beauty of the bird with his own worldly renunciation in such a way that "he cannot decisively judge between them, and holds both with agony in his mind." Such a painful ambiguity of attitude is illustrated by Empson, using the N.E.D.

Buckle admits of two tenses and two meanings: "they do buckle here," or "come, and buckle yourself here"; *buckle* like a military belt, for the discipline of heroic action, and *buckle* like a bicycle wheel, "make useless, distorted, and incapable of its natural motion." ... *Chevalier* personifies either physical or spiritual activity; Christ riding to Jerusalem, or the Cavalryman ready for the charge; Pegasus, or the Windhover.

Frequently, Empson uses alternative paraphrases of a line to suggest the multiple readings possible when the syntax is uncertain. Quoting Yeats's poem beginning "Who will go drive with Fergus now,/ And pierce the deep wood's woven shade,"

[11]

Empson concentrates on the adverb "now" to show the importance to meaning of this pivotal word. The "now" may mean before Fergus abandons his courtly activities for the contemplative ones of the Druids, or after he does so. "If after, the first line means: 'Now that the awful example of Fergus is in front of you, surely you will not be so unwise as to brood?' If before . . . then . . . the first line gives: 'Who will come out with the great figures of the Court, and join in their sensible out-of-door pleasures?'" The full Empsonian treatment of a passage, however, can be readily observed in his analysis of Donne's "A Valediction of Weeping," which, he says, "weeps for two reasons." Empson rings the changes from dictionary definitions, through artful and exhaustive paraphrasing, through analysis of syntax and punctuation to a penetrating, yet debatable, psychological interpretation of Donne's mixed feelings on his departure from his beloved. Donne, Empson concludes, kept his feelings ambiguous "because he felt that at such a time it would be ungenerous to spread them out clearly in his mind."

Critics of Empson, sometimes less generous than he, have vociferously rejected many of his variant readings as well as his psychologizing. They have pointed with persistency to Empson's sometimes careless treatment of texts—his misquotations and textual errors—or to his preoccupations with the dictionary. To some of his critics, Empson's verbal analysis is at best offhanded, slightly wrongheaded perhaps, or perverse at worst, but especially regrettable, they feel, is his reluctance to evaluate, to judge the work of literature he examines. *Seven Types*, perhaps because it is best known, or most illustrative of his method, has been frequently castigated. The examples cited from Hopkins, Yeats, or Donne may reveal some of these weaknesses, but they also show the particular value and strength of Empson's exegeses. To students and poets, even to average readers, who avoid entanglements with Empson's seven types or

[12]

who are unconcerned with textual slips, the analyses are helpful and stimulating, frequently witty. They provoke the reader into reading carefully; they challenge him to accept or deny the multiple renderings of words and lines, forcing on him the same fierce commitment to meaning that Empson exhibits. For such heady pleasures, or hardy responsibilities, the book is dipped into and used.

Answering his critics, in the *Kenyon Review*, and stating his credo of verbal analysis, Empson stoutly maintains that final evaluation of a literary text is "merely irrelevant" in his kind of criticism.

There is room for a great deal of exposition, in which the business of the critic is simply to show how the machine is meant to work, and therefore to show all its working parts in turn. This is the kind of criticism I am especially interested in, and I think it is often really needed.

Empson is characteristically exploratory and suggestive in his exposition, showing how the machine works. But if the more pontifical value judgments of many critics are absent, there is present in his writings a constant sense of pleasure and admiration. Less a mechanic than a jeweler, say, Empson reveals implicit value judgment as he goes about displaying the precision works of literary timepieces. He examines those passages which puzzle or delight him. While the analytical technique he employs may be wasted on trivia, Empson is never wasteful. At times, however, he may seem to avoid deciding on the relevance of definitions or alternative interpretations, and his procedures may become tedious or exhausting. He sometimes recognizes this difficulty, for, as he says on one occasion, "the machinery of interpretation is becoming too cumbrous here."

Attracted often to the difficult poem which elicits involved explanation, Empson can also write movingly and convincingly about uncomplicated lyrics. One of the more eloquent passages

[13]

in *Seven Types* is his analysis of a sestine from Sidney's *Arcadia*. It also reveals Empson's quiet and sensitive appraisal of a piece of literature. After tracing the meanings of the six recurring words (*mountaines, vallies, forrests, musique, evening, morning*), he comments on the way repetitions and variations of them slowly build up interest.

So that when the static conception of the complaint has been finally brought into light . . . a whole succession of feelings about the local scenery . . . has been enlisted into sorrow and beats as a single passion of the mind. I have put this poem at the end of a discussion ostensibly about rhythm, and shall mention its rhythm only to remark that it is magnificent.

Seven Types presents and tests out the Empsonian method of verbal analysis as applied primarily to brief selections from longer works, or to an occasional sonnet or short lyric. Empson's second book, *Some Versions of Pastoral*, puts the method to work on an extended scale and is concerned with larger portions or whole works. It is, like *Seven Types*, a septet of variations on a predominant theme. Beginning with an unconventional analysis of proletarian literature, Empson works through to a definition of pastoral as the "process of putting the complex into the simple." The remaining six versions are arranged "roughly in historical order," as he examines the pastoral theme with attendant social ideas. Empson admits candidly that his examples are more surprising than normal or expected. Once started on an example, obviously selected in a highly individualistic manner, he tends to disregard the unity of the book. The uncertain result, he says, is not "a solid piece of sociology." "But I should claim," he adds, "that the same trick of thought, taking very different forms, is followed through a historical series."

The series includes a surprising and ingenious array of "pastorals"— Elizabethan drama, Shakespeare's *Troilus and Cressida*,

Donne's poetry (particularly Holy Sonnet V and "The Cross"), Shakespeare's Sonnet 94, Marvell's "The Garden," Milton's *Paradise Lost*, Gay's *The Beggar's Opera*, and Lewis Carroll's *Alice in Wonderland* and *Through the Looking Glass*. Scattered throughout the book are brief quotations from a variety of English writers, but Shakespeare, Donne, and Marvell are most frequently cited. *Some Versions* reveals Empson's continuing concern with verbal complexities, metaphysical conceits, and the multiple meanings of words. Characteristic is his catalogue of Marvell's use of "green," and his calculation that the first line of Shakespeare's Sonnet 94 yields 4,906 "possible movements of thought."

The chapters on Marvell, Gay, and Lewis Carroll seem the best in the book. Empson's approach to Marvell's "The Garden" is his familiar one of verbal analysis, broadened, now, to include the sociological and historical bias of the book. Declaring that the poem is about the contrast and reconciliation of "conscious and unconscious states, intuitive and intellectual modes of apprehension," Empson paraphrases Marvell's well-known couplet "Annihilating all that's made/ To a green thought in a green shade."

"Either 'reducing the whole material world to nothing material, *i.e.* to a green thought,' or 'considering the material world as of no value compared to a green thought'"; either contemplating everything or shutting everything out.

Both extreme consciousness ("including everything because understanding it") and extreme animality ("including everything because in harmony with it") are combined for Empson in the extraordinary inclusiveness of the couplet. No wonder that he views such a paradoxically contradictory condition as ecstatically like the Buddhist seventh state of enlightenment. The seventh ambiguity could do no more. It is Empson's conclusion that only a metaphysical poet such as Marvell could so effectively dramatize the mind's complex relation to Nature. As a critic, Empson probes Marvell's technique, analyzing what he considers the poet's concerns with unifying the antitheses of consciousness and unconsciousness, "perception and creation, the one and the many." Empson's own stylized poetry will often attempt the same sort of reconciliation.

Empson's discussion of *The Beggar's Opera* points to the mock-pastoral, or the "resolution of heroic and pastoral into a cult of independence." The roguery of Macheath, the villainy of Peachum, and the seriocomic affairs of Polly are used by Empson for a provocative examination of the Tory Augustan's attitudes toward man and society, toward aristocrats, rogues, and Whigs. His witty, penetrating asides, sociological and political, add spice, seasoning a well-ordered essay. Less ordered, but certainly well seasoned, is Empson's analysis of Carroll's Alice ("The Child as Swain").

Since Alice's stories are so clearly about growing up, says Empson, it is appropriate to translate them into Freudian terms, to make the analysis psychoanalysis. The result, notable for its clarity and balance, should be the model for those critics hectically following Freud's way through the dark labyrinths in the creative unconscious. Empson, unlike many who place authors or characters on the couch, does not concern himself with a "neurosis peculiar to Dodgson," that shy Cambridge mathematician whose pathetic attraction to girl children led eventually to the Alice books. Rather, Empson uses Freud where appropriate for a discussion of the unselfconsciously sexy child who judges society through "the clear but blank eyes of sexlessness."

Radiating out from the basic Freudian interpretation (Alice's fall through a hole into Mother Earth, her birth trauma, keyless condition, concern for the rabbit's phallic pencil, and her troubles with the passionate Queen of Hearts) are a series of provocative observations on nineteenth-century literature, social conventions, politics, and industrial economy. Empson delights and astounds, whether he is tracing the development of the Romantic child-cult back to the Cromwellian Civil War, puritanism, and the end of dueling, or whether he is claiming "moral grandeur" for the White Knight because "he stands for the Victorian Scientist, who was felt to have invented a new kind of Roman virtue." Never dull, the chapter on Alice is an invigorating and witty piece of writing, but a cluttered and disorganized one. Its sheer prolixity of brilliant observations mitigates against tidiness, yet it is always readable. The chapter proves Empson superior to Joyce's "grisly old Sykos" who, in *Finnegans Wake*, did their "unsmiling bit on' alices, when they were yung and easily freudened."

The Structure of Complex Words, Empson's third book of criticism, is perhaps his most solemn and ambitious undertaking to date. It is as complex as its title suggests. A lengthy, difficult analysis of literary language, it relies heavily upon theories of value and language derived from I. A. Richards, but carefully modified by Empson to provide a study of his specific cases. Once more the range of the illustrative examples from literature is impressive, but *Complex Words* also draws frequently upon the writings of linguists, psychologists, anthropologists, philosophers, and historians, making it the most learned of Empson's books. Combining theory with analytical criticism, the book is, as Empson admits, a "sandwich"; the criticism is the meat of the matter at center. Two introductory chapters on feelings and statements in words (categorical Empson finds five types of statements), and seven concluding chapters, more or less theoretical, hold in between the solid matter of twelve analytical chapters. As in the two previous books, examples from Shakespeare provide the most substance. Four plays—*Lear, Timon of Athens, Othello, Measure for Measure*—receive extended examination. The words upon which Empson concentrates, through the twelve chapters, are "wit," "all," "fool," "dog" (rogue), "honest," "sense," and "sensibility." It is somehow comforting to realize that there are seven of these major words.

From "wit" to "sensibility," the words, for Empson, are complex because they have "structures" of meaning built up in a particular social or historical context recognizable both to writer and to audience. In *Complex Words*, he goes beyond his examination of artfully manipulated ambiguities in a passage to concentrate on the "key" word in a long work of literature. By singling out such a centrally important word for analysis, Empson attempts to interpret or open up the work by means of the word. Selection of a convincing *passe partout* is essential, as well as the adroit use of the N.E.D. His investigations of the hierarchies of meanings attached to "wit" in Pope's *Essay on Criticism*, to "fool" in *King Lear*, or to "honest" in *Othello* serve admirably and wittily to illuminate these works.

Having approached Pope's *Essay* "rather coolly," in search of crude examples to prove his thesis on the structure of meaning, Empson admits, "I now think that the analysis improves the poem a good deal, and indeed shows how it was meant to be read." The meaningful structure Empson sees in Pope's "wit" reveals more about eighteenth-century attitudes which the poet accepted and played upon than it does of Pope's final opinions. "The cleverness of the thing is that the epigrams are irrefutable if you stretch the meanings of the words far enough and give what the age demanded if you let them slip back." "Wit" appears once every sixteen lines in the *Essay*, says Empson, and he proceeds to trace the possible meanings with his favorite authority, the dictionary. He believes that Pope in using the word was striking a balance between Longinus and Horace, between the sublime use which thrills and the epigrammatic use which causes fools and wise men alike to admire or approve. The use of the word even approaches Coleridge's use of Imagination. Pope's man of wit, as Empson delineates him, may be "1. bright social talker 2. critic of the arts or of society 3. poet or artist." In any role, he may be "a. mocking, b. acting as judge, c. giving aesthetic pleasure or expressing new truths." Context, tone, and mood, the essence of style, determine the "equations . . . between these meanings." Probably the most nearly complete "equation," where the structure of meaning is most admirable, is found by Empson in lines 233–238 of the *Essay*. The man of wit, in these lines, acts as the "perfect Judge" who retains "The generous pleasure to be charmed with Wit."

Empson, with customary candor, admits his heavy indebtedness to A. C. Bradley for his general interpretations of Shakespeare, but he invariably goes beyond Bradley in his pursuit of a word's contextual significance. He examines the forty-seven appearances of "fool" in *King Lear*, for example, or those of "honest" in *Othello*.

The fifty-two uses of *honest* and *honesty* in *Othello* are a very queer business; there is no other play in which Shakespeare worries a word like that. *King Lear* uses *fool* nearly as often but does not treat it as a puzzle, only as a source of profound metaphors.

What makes the business queer, and Shakespeare worrisome, it seems, is that the Bard must have hated a peculiar use of "honest" which was "at once hearty and individualistic, which was then common among raffish low people but did not become upperclass til the Restoration." Putting together the structure of such a word in such a play is complicated by its changing meaning.

At some stage of the development . . . the word came to have in it a covert assertion that the man who accepts the natural desires, who does not live by principle, will be fit for such warm uses of *honest* as imply "generous" and "faithful to friends," and to believe this is to disbelieve the Fall of Man.

Less rewarding than Empson's analyses of words from Pope or Shakespeare is his discussion of Milton's "all" in *Paradise*

[19]

Lost, probably because the key word is less significant than "wit," "fool," or "honest." The danger inherent in this method of analysis, not always avoided by Empson, is that much of the poetry and part of the sense may be lost from the whole. One word, no matter how skillfully chosen and used, may not be the best key after all. It may never unlock anything more than an anteroom. As in his other books, Empson's anecdotal knowledge of history and manners, his cleverly challenging or offhand comments, provide much of the pleasure to be derived from reading *Complex Words.* The scholarship is sounder and more obvious in this book than in Empson's others, but in spite of so much apparently objective documentation, the judgments are frequently subjective. The reader, agreeing or disagreeing with them, nevertheless probably finds them stimulating.

Critical reception of *Complex Words* was, Empson thought, often obtuse or mean-minded. One critic claimed it was a solemn joke. In a letter to *Mandrake* (Autumn-Winter, 1955–56), however, Empson refutes his critics. Stating his sense of elation and achievement over the completed work, and extending his metaphors, he calls it an airplane:

A certain amount of noisy taxi-ing round the field at the start may be admitted, and the landing at the end is bumpy though I think without causing damage; but the power of the thing and the view during its flight I consider magnificent.

At least one critic, Richard Sleight, believes *Complex Words* to be Empson's best book, as important for its time as Eliot's *The Sacred Wood.* Moreover, it was during the time of its composition in Peking that Empson ceased writing poetry, apparently finding in the creative labors of that massive, complex work of criticism a satisfaction denied him in his poetry. Until the canon of his work is complete, *Complex Words* would appear to be the high point of Empson's criticism. In contrast, his later book, *Milton's God* (1961), is a less significant work.

Empson's writing on Milton's *Paradise Lost* has grown over the years from the few, casual observations in *Seven Types*, the essay on pastoral in *Some Versions*, and the brief examination of one word in *Complex Words*, finally to an entire book on Milton's major poem. Controversial, unabashedly anti-Christian, *Milton's God* has provoked heated critical reaction. The book presents Empson's challenging reading of Milton in seven chapters, if not seven types, which deal successively with critics, Satan, Heaven, Eve, Adam, Delilah in *Samson Agonistes*, and Christianity. Asserting his belief that the Christian God is wicked, a belief he says he held as a Cambridge undergraduate, Empson sets about examining how Milton succeeds in making God "noticeably less wicked than the traditional Christian one." Says Empson, "I thus tend to accept the details of interpretation which various recent critics have used to prove the poem bad and then try to show that they make it good." His emphasis on what he views as the cruelties, iniquities, and absurdities of Christianity is an important part of his critical approach to *Paradise Lost*.

As usual, Empson's wit and lively intelligence make his readings of the text thoroughly engaging even when they seem most outrageous. There is always a sense of play in the midst of high seriousness, so that the cerebrations and speculations are gay as well as provocative. Milton's Satan, declares Empson for example, is both a "conscientious republican" and a "rippingly grand aristocrat," which makes him like a Yorkshireman or a Norman baron with complicated loyalties to the throne. Satan's questioning of God's autocratic power, however, reminds Empson of a "Professor doubting the credentials of his Vice-Chancellor." The punishment which follows is out of all proportion, thinks professor Empson. God may be like a Vice-Chancellor, but He is also like "King Lear and Prospero, turbulent and masterful characters who are struggling to become able to renounce their power and enter peace." Most alarming of all, God, like "Uncle Joe" Stalin, has "the same patience under an appearance of roughness, the same flashes of joviality, the same thorough unscrupulousness, the same real bad temper."

For some readers, particularly those concerned with Empson's poetry, *Milton's God* is likely to be of interest less for what it says about Milton than for what it says about Empson. More personal and anecdotal than his other three books of criticism, it proves a mine of Empsoniana. Of late, he has returned to Shakespearean studies and the literature which inaugurated his undergraduate critical activities. In crackling book reviews and typically loquacious articles, he continues his lively, individualistic dialogue on the Bard.

Empson's influence on modern literary criticism has been important, even if he is thought of, all too frequently, as the author of only one book. Influential he is, and yet he is too independent and individualistic to have fostered a "school" of criticism, or to have inspired protégés. His critical approach to literature, however, under the various labels of verbal analysis, formalistic, ontological, or contextual criticism, has been most frequently related to the American "new criticism." Whether "new" or not, it is characterized by the close reading of texts, with attention to paradoxical or ambiguous use of language. The "new critics," comprising John Crowe Ransom, Allen Tate, Cleanth Brooks, and others, have been a remarkably influential and congenial group of scholars, critics, and poets. Their endeavors include establishing such prestigious periodicals as the *Southern Review, Sewanee Review,* and *Kenyon Review.* Empson has published frequently in these quarterlies, he has twice taught in the Kenyon College Summer School (1948, 1950), and he seems to be acquainted with many of the critics. While they usually are receptive, though sometimes critical, of Empson's methods, their development has been separate, or perhaps parallel to his. They, like Empson, are partially indebted to the precepts of Eliot and Richards.

Empson has never been an active member of any critical school, nor has he been associated with the influential English group which developed around F. R. Leavis at Cambridge, and *Scrutiny* magazine. Although Empson knew Leavis at Cambridge, and published two early articles in *Scrutiny*, he has practiced a form of criticism at odds with the moralizing, evaluative work of the *Scrutiny* group. Praising his early poetry, Leavis has been sharply critical of both the later poetry and the criticism. Empson, in turn, has gaily satirized Leavis in a poem, "Your Teeth Are Ivory Towers."

As a critic, Empson has upheld the importance and usefulness of analysis, an examination of parts and functions leading to understanding. Although he can and does write sensitively about the simple lyric, he is clearly attracted to poetry which permits, even requires, much tinkering with the machinery. As a poet, Empson has stated his poetic credo which reveals his admiration for poems with conventional, but complicated, parts. Ambiguity of statement and complexity of analogy and structure are the grist for his own mill. "I am in favor of rhyme and metre in English poetry," says Empson, declaring his beliefs in the *British Journal of Aesthetics*. Criticizing free verse, he maintains the need in poetry for strict meters and the "singing line." Imagism, like vers libre, is bad because it lacks control; it is, he says, "determindedly anti-intellectual, and tells us that we ought to try to be very stupid." He maintains that arguing in verse is wonderfully poetic. To argue poetically, with or without a "singing line," is to exercise logical control not only over the statement of the poem but also over the selection of imagery. Rationally and self-consciously using imagery, arguing, putting rhythm, rhyme, and meter at the service of the intellect, is to write poetry in a manner reminiscent of seventeenth-century poetry.

[23]

This manner, and the wit which enlivens Empson's poetry, prove it similar in some ways to the poetry of John Donne and the metaphysicals.

There can be no doubt about Empson's conscious attempt to write poetry like John Donne, although his success in doing so may be questioned. Empson several times has confessed his direct indebtedness to the metaphysical poets. He amusingly admits to Christopher Ricks that, as an undergraduate, "I thought it would be very nice to write beautiful things like the poet Donne. I would sit by the fire trying to think of an interesting puzzle." The twentieth-century revival of interest in metaphysical poetry, which so moved Empson to inspiration and imitation, is traceable to H. J. C. Grierson's two-volume edition of Donne's poetry (1912), his anthology *Metaphysical Lyrics and Poems of the Seventeenth Century* (1921), and to T. S. Eliot's "The Metaphysical Poets" (1921), an essay on the Grierson anthology. Eliot's further articles on Marvell, Donne, and Crashaw proved influential. Many young poets during the 1920s and early 1930s, when Empson was writing his first poems, were under the double influence of Eliot and the metaphysicals. What Empson and others gained from a study of the metaphysicals, and Eliot's particular view of their practice, was respect for wit, learned metaphors, and passionately intellectualized emotions.

Learned wit, employed by any writer from Shakespeare to Swift, from Joyce to Beckett, may satirize, provoking mirth or outrage, or it may suggest astonishing connections between dissimilar areas of experience. Not all learned wit, however, is metaphysical. Technique as well as attitude particularizes the poetry of those who are metaphysically witty. The recurring uses of antithesis, paradox, pun, and conceit mark such poetry. Linking different domains through these devices, exercising logical organization, and intellectualizing the emotions, metaphysical poetry attempts to constrain an exploding universe. The metaphysical conceit, an extended analogy, is perhaps the most obvious device for bridging the gaps in a fragmenting world order. Drawn from such diverse and traditionally "unpoetic" disciplines as mathematics, physics, biology, astronomy, even machine technology, the witty conceit reveals the poet's learning and logic. Elliot maintained that metaphysicals deliberately searched for an intellectual equivalent of an emotion, finding it, like Donne, in conceits employing astronomy, alchemy, geography, or geometry.

Empson's conceits, typically drawn from mathematics and science, help hold his world together. Because the mathematics and science he uses are frequently post-Newtonian, his analogies also communicate modern man's precarious existence in a non-Euclidean, Einsteinian universe. Many of the early poems, those published in *Poems* (1935), turn on such analogies. "The World's End," for example, proving that there is no end to space or man's predicament, merely a new beginning, utilizes concepts of curved and expanding space together with those from geometry, calculus, and relativity theory. Empson's use of Einstein, and the new physics as popularized by Sir Arthur Eddington, is particularly effective in a love poem which echoes Marvell's "The Definition of Love." Like the seventeenth-century poets, Empson in "The World's End" makes his analogy of space-time central to his witty proposal, exploring the possibilities of the conceit with marvelous logic. Equally central to "Letter I" is another conceit drawing on the Eddingtonian, expanding, curviliear universe. Further reference to non-Euclidean geometry, networks of space which are pointless, suggest the difficulties of modern lovers trying to communicate with one another or to share a common experience.

Traditional geometry often provides Empson with such conceits as the locus-line-tangent-envelope analogy in "Letter V," or the focus-line-ellipse analogy in "Dissatisfaction with Metaphysics." In both poems Empson adds optical analogies from classical physics to the geometrical ones. Chemical or biochemical conceits are used in both "Villanelle" and "Missing Dates" to describe the toxic reactions of the lover-poet to the poisons of lost love or to missed opportunities. His most extensive chemical analogy, however, is in "Bacchus" where the processes of distillation and inebriation are worked out with witty exactitude. Parasitology and botany provide Empson with his ingenious liver fluke analogy for the Japanese invasion in "China," and with the beautifully sustained conceit of the phoenixlike conifer from Turkestan in "Note on Local Flora."

Occasionally, Empson will turn to nonscientific, nonmathematical knowledge for his metaphors, as in "Legal Fiction" where law makes much out of the "short stakes of men," but even in this poem Empson's penchant for the geometrical and scientific considerably complicates the basic legal analogy. As his style and subject matter change in the later poems, those published in *The Gathering Storm* (1940), Empson's use of the metaphysical conceit diminishes, but he never completely abandons his interest in the logically extended, learned analogy. Empson's easy familiarity with scientific and mathematical terms, his pervasive use of them in the early poems, and his manner of frequently making them functional parts of the whole characterize him as perhaps the most "scientific" of twentieth-century poets.

The thought and emotion Empson communicates in his first book of poetry, *Poems* (1935), evolve from concerns which are partly traditional and partly the result of contemporary problems. If his poems are about "the young man feeling frightened, frightened of women, frightened of jobs, frightened of everything, not knowing what he could possibly do," as he told Christopher Ricks in an interview, they are also about failures of communication, the difficulty of maintaining traditional beliefs, the isolation of the individual, and the unresolved dilemmas of doing and knowing, of thinking and feeling. Notably, the poems are not about the class struggle, about politics, nor about any of the socioeconomic concerns so frequently found in the poetry of the thirties. Although the volume appeared the year before the outbreak of the Spanish Civil War, it clearly did not reflect the tenor of the times. The mid-1930s in British literature was marked by a relatively strong Marxist influence. Auden, Isherwood, Day Lewis, Spender, MacNeice, and others often lyrically celebrated Lenin, Marx, and workingmen. Empson, while perhaps sympathizing with the "Auden Group" in social or political matters, never wrote like them. Nor did he write like the surrealists, then active, whose dreamlike metaphors and avowedly antirationalistic procedures were in marked contrast to the strenuous logic of Empson's metaphysical conceits. Dylan Thomas, for all the apparently surrealistic qualities of some of his early poems, was producing his strongly individualistic poetry at this time which reveals some metaphysical qualities. But neither his exuberant rhetoric nor his proliferating, luxurious imagery is anything like Empson's. As a poet, he is not Empson's sort. Among young poets of the 1930s, Empson stands alone, as distinct in his way as Auden or Thomas, but less popular and less influential.

The volume of *Collected Poems* conveniently brings together all but a few of Empson's published poems, exactly duplicating the ordering of poems from his two volumes—*Poems* and *The Gathering Storm*. The dividing point between the two is "Bacchus," the thirty-first poem in the collected edition. All but ten of the poems appearing in the first volume were undergraduate poems, first published in the Cambridge magazines. Two remarkable, even unique, aspects of the first volume are retained in the *Collected Poems*—the quoted text of Buddha's "Fire Sermon," unexplained at the beginning of the book, and the many pages of "Notes" at the end. Both suggest the influence of T. S. Eliot's *The Waste Land* (1922).

The third part of Eliot's poem is entitled "The Fire Sermon." It concludes with quoted fragments from the "Sermon" as well as from St. Augustine's *Confessions* which emphasize the theme of self-destructive sterile lust. Empson's enigmatic use of the "Sermon," however, seems to suggest more than a timely reminder of man's sexual or spiritual predicament in a modern wasteland. Throughout his prose, but particularly in *Seven Types* (under the seventh ambiguity) and in *Some Versions*, Empson refers to the Buddhistic reconciliation of opposites, the avoidance of life's extremes of either self-torture or self-indulgence, through following the noble eightfold path to Nirvana. In many of the poems Empson struggles to define and state the middle way, for, as he declares in his note to "Bacchus," "life involves maintaining oneself between contradictions that can't be solved by analysis." The "Sermon," therefore, is of undeniable importance to Empson's early poems. The imaginative, yet precarious and probably impossible, resolution of polarities is one of his pervasive themes.

Empson probably owes as much to Pope as to Eliot for the origin of his kind of annotated poem. Avoiding the slightly pontifical or solemn tone of Eliot's much-discussed *Waste Land* notes, Empson's own are not unlike the dryly humorous, ironical, exegetical notes added to the *Dunciad Variorum*. Never providing exact documentation, Empson's notes, while explanatory, are often self-contained. Contrapuntal in effect, usually providing another dimension to the poem, they expand the meaning, or add the pleasures of prose to poetry. He calls them "prose bridges" to the poems, providing answers to their puzzles. The saving grace is Empson's ironic, casual tone and his unpretentious, yet teasing, declaration that the Notes are possible admissions of failure, that "the better poems tend to require fewer notes."

One of the characteristic, and well-annotated, poems in Empson's first volume is "Arachne." It is also a compelling example of Empson's use of Buddha's advice about extremes. In the first two stanzas, "Arachne" provides an exploration of the human condition in the most general terms.

> Twixt devil and deep sea, man hacks his caves;
> Birth, death; one, many; what is true, and seems;
> Earth's vast hot iron, cold space's empty waves:
>
> King spider, walks the velvet roof of streams:
> Must bird and fish, must god and beast avoid:
> Dance, like nine angels, on pin-point extremes.

The extremes are stated with variations. Birth and death, one and many, appearance and reality are the opposite absolutes of life, as well as of philosophy. Speculation about them, we learn from another poem ("Dissatisfaction with Metaphysics"), is incestuous and fruitless. Man's position, like the spider's, must be the middle ground between hell and heaven; it must be between the physical types of birds and fish, and between godlike knowledge and bestial mindlessness.

The regal arachnid mentioned in stanza two is Arachne, but perhaps it is also Christ or Everyman. Empson comments in *Some Versions:* "The supreme example of the problem of the One and Many was given by the Logos who was an individual man." Representing man, King Christ may be thought to resolve both the antinomies of philosophy and the disparities of God and beast. Arachne, of course, was the human whose disastrously presumptuous pride led her to challenge a goddess. Failing to avoid one extreme, she was reduced to spidery existence. Outside of myth, reducing man to spider may be satirical and disparaging. But because Arachne, after her transformation, successfully dangles "between void and void," she is the perfect exemplar for muddling man who is caught in the middle. Empson's ingenious, yet unpleasant, analogy suggests a complex vision of man's pride, courage, and virtue which avoids the extreme of pure satire.

Turning from the resolution of life's dangerous opposites in the opening stanzas of "Arachne," Empson concludes his poem by particularizing the problem in terms of a love affair. In true metaphysical fashion, elaborating on an analogy from science, he uses the surface tension and molecular structure of a bubble to signify the delicate, interdependent relationship of lovers. Empson reminds the modern, vain Arachne of his poem that she is not self-sufficient, and that the male is necessary. Only between the two of them can the bubble of existence be maintained, for, as he says, "Male spiders must not be too early slain." Destroying the male creates a dangerous imbalance which leads, obviously, to one of the extremes which men, or spiders, must avoid. If king-spider-man and his tightrope walk between opposites is the subject of the poem, it is addressed to his Arachne, a well-known disturber of equilibrium. Progressing from an essay on man to an essay on love, Empson's poem ends as a clever, if nervous, request for amatory coexistence. It reveals more than merely a young man being frightened of women.

"Arachne," when Empson published it in the *Cambridge Review* of June, 1928, was only his ninth poem to appear, but already he had established his customary tone, style, and content. Using terza rima, he defies expectations by exploiting an early traditional form (taken from Dante's *Commedia* and employed by Shelley in "Ode to the West Wind") in an untraditional manner. The interlocking stanzas serve Empson admirably to convey the impression of a continuing, unresolvable human dilemma, but talk of surface tension, molecules, and the sexual pleasures of cannibalistic spiders is hardly what Dante had in mind when he used the form. It is Empson who is among the first modern poets to rework the old stanzaic patterns incorporating contemporary concerns. His new wine in old bottles, however, is sometimes rather vinegary. Likewise, the villanelle, that involved and restrictive early French form, will never be the same since Empson took it over. Poets like Auden, Dylan Thomas, and the "movement" poets of the 1950s seem particularly indebted to him for their awareness of both terza rima and the villanelle.

In all, Empson has written three villanelles, "Villanelle," "Missing Dates," and "Reflection from Anita Loos." Aside from the last one, a disturbing and disappointing poem, his villanelles are skillful manipulations of the form. The form imposes the strict limitations of a repetitive rhyme scheme, with only two rhymes throughout the nineteen-line poem, and the alternate recurrence of the first and third lines in each successive stanza. Subtle variations of emphasis are possible, but difficult, as in Dylan Thomas's splendid and ardent "Do Not Go Gentle into That Good Night." Empson's "Villanelle" is exemplary, if not as magnificently rhetorical as Thomas's poem.

"Villanelle" displays a closely reasoned analysis of the familiar paradox of love's disease—the medicine that poisons, or the cure that kills. The sciences involved are medicine, chemistry, and alchemy, but Empson's analogies are ultimately less metaphysical than traditional.

> It is the pain, it is the pain, endures.
> Your chemic beauty burned my muscles through.
> Poise of my hands reminded me of yours.

Each line of the first stanza contains one of the three most important words in the poem—pain, chemic, and poise. Between the pain which endures and the poise which reminds, the chemic beauty of the girl is the pivotal element, at once the cause of the infection and its possible cure. References to "deep toxin" and "poison draft" in subsequent stanzas support the reading. (For a similar poison draft see Shakespeare's 119th sonnet.) The girl's beauty is appropriately ambiguous, however, for if it is poisonous, it is also a "deep beauty," which is allied with "kindness" and "grace" in other stanzas. The final curative powers of the lady are questionable. Under such circumstances, it is understandable why the pain endures.

The remarkable third line of the poem, repeated three times as form requires, remains enigmatic and challenges ingenuity. "Poise" may mean weight, balance, manner, or bearing. In what sense the lover's hands have such poise is not certain. Perhaps they form a gesture of indifference, submission, or despair. They may also carry the tactile sensation of previous caresses, reminding the lover of the girl's physical beauty. Hands are obviously important. The present tense of "endures" and the past tense of "reminded" seem to imply that, however hopeful the "poise" may be, its efficacy fades before that unremittent pain.

The poem closes without hope. While the girl's beauty and kindness are unchanged, her shape the same, she is ultimately remote. The love affair is inconclusive. "You are still kind whom the same shape immures./ Kind and beyond adieu. We miss our cue." If the memory of her persists, she is beyond "adieu," for the lover has somehow been unable to come in when he should to complete the relationship, or to be completely cured. Like Prufrock, who was also concerned with hands, Empson's lover has perhaps seen the moment of his greatness flicker. If he is no Hamlet, neither is he Othello. Unlike tragic heroes, he has missed his cue, and the affair hangs in the balance, poised painfully between exits and entrances.

"Missing Dates," published nine years after "Villanelle" and collected in the second volume of poetry, *The Gathering*

[32]

Storm, is no less polished in form than the earlier poem, but it is freer of elaborate conceits. The imagery and tone are distinctly different from traditional villanelles, although the theme may not be so remote from the genre as at first appears. More open, and perhaps more convincing in the emotional quality of its statements than "Villanelle," it is one of Empson's best-known poems. It is partly, if not wholly, about lost poems, as the last stanza explains.

> It is the poems you have lost, the ills
> From missing dates, at which the heart expires.
> Slowly the poison the whole blood stream fills.
> The waste remains, the waste remains and kills.

Whether misplaced, undiscovered, or unfinished, these dates and poems represent missed opportunities. If such timely and creative moments are missed, or misspent in life, the sad result is often a remorseful death. This outcome of unseized time has been the chill moral of innumerable poems by poets who, taking to heart Horace's advice, *Carpe diem*, have known what to do with rosebuds, girls, and golden hours. Whether the mistress or the Muse is coy, the poet has been aware of the yawning grave and time's hurrying chariot.

Somber, slow, and sorrowful, the rhythm of "Missing Dates" contributes effectively to the mood and underscores the meaning. Poisons and waste products, the results of missed moments, gradually cause the death of the heart or spirit. What makes the poem impressive is the sense of inevitability connected with the process so skillfully conveyed through rhythm, tone, and imagery. The harrowing awareness of inescapable destruction is moving. The title, by calling attention to dates, reminds the reader that time tells.

Approaching death, but not death of the heart, is the subject of "To an Old Lady," another one of Empson's most anthologized poems. It has often been praised for its combination of metaphysical wit and deep, personal feeling. Whether or not his mother is the subject of the poem, the moon is metaphor, and Empson's parallel allows him just the right distance from his subject for objectivity. The praise and admiration for this gallant lady may seem, therefore, gently ironic.

> Ripeness is all; her in her cooling planet
> Revere; do not presume to think her wasted.
> Project her no projectile, plan nor man it;

Rather, he says, man your telescope to observe her: "Watch while her ritual is still to see,/ Still stand her temples emptying in the sand." Edgar in *King Lear* said that "Ripeness is all," and Edgar's ripeness is Hamlet's readiness—a fortitude in the face of death or disaster. Ripeness is also the perfection of a past. Empson's ripeness means all of these, and is the reason we are not to pity the lady as the chill of death approaches. As a moon goddess she is to be revered. We are not to assume that so full a moon is decayed, nor that her significance is unappreciated. The irony, however, is that in fact she wanes; her rituals are passing, her temples emptying, her crops failing.

The planetary metaphor is handled impressively by Empson, who uses it metaphysically to structure the poem. But more than the lady's gentility or her moribundity is suggested by the analogy. Regal, aloof, and self-sufficient, she is mistress of her social rituals. She displays "Wit used to run a house and to play Bridge,/ And tragic fervour, to dismiss her maids." If Empson praises her wit, poise, strength, and serenity, he especially pays homage to her style. She lives and dies with flair in a world which increasingly makes meaningful action difficult if not impossible.

Throughout his poetry, Empson displays a continuing concern for style, for form, for the intricacies of manners and behavior which may allow one to survive in an Einsteinian world with a measure of grace. His despairing, witty advice in "This Last Pain" is to pretend and to act as if action were of value, to "build an edifice of form/ For house where phantoms may keep warm."

> Imagine, then, by miracle with me,
> (Ambiguous gifts, as what gods give must be)
> What could not possibly be there,
> And learn a style from a despair.

Man's despair, and Empson's, is the "last pain" of mental or spiritual anguish, far worse than the physical. In Christian theology, as Dante and Boethius knew, it is reserved for those damned souls who are able to understand, but not to experience, the ultimate, beatific bliss of God. In secular terms such bliss resides in a system of values or beliefs which are no longer possible. Modern man is painfully conscious of his desires and tortured by his frustrated expectations. Cut away from his beliefs by scientific, rationalistic knowledge, man is faced with the problem of retaining empty values and of pretending that they mean something. The agonizing reality of contemporary life can only be faced with stylish despair, with an "edifice of form," which may not lead to salvation but may transform the pain to something resembling grace.

The illusions necessary to life which are so desperately and knowingly preserved are created and maintained by the imagination, an "ambiguous gift" to be sure. Ludwig Wittgenstein, mentioned in the poem, and the Logical Positivists, as well as modern mathematical physics, have emptied the beliefs and caused man to whistle stylishly in the dark of his hell. Illusions, in such desperate circumstances, may be all that anyone has left. Like Stein's "destructive element" in Conrad's *Lord Jim*, they paradoxically may save as they destroy.

"Legal Fiction" is a poem which chronicles another of man's illusions, the legal fiction that he who owns the soil also owns the sky above and the depths beneath. In this example, law extends the "short stakes" of men into "long spokes." Empson characteristically satirizes intellectual *hubris* which leads to deluded rationalizations over man's all too earthbound limitations. There is a curious exhilaration in Empson's legal and geometrical metaphors, however, which transcends despair. The fictions may be untrue and improbable, but they tend to exalt the power of the conceiving mind. As in other poems, Empson seems in "Legal Fiction" both to admire and to decry such mental dexterity. If man's intellectual pride leads to his downfall ("the lighthouse beam you own/ Flashes like Lucifer, through the firmament"), there is something splendid in his failure. In an age of uncertainties, such fictions are at least as true as other beliefs, and often comforting besides.

Among the many uncertainties analyzed in *Poems*, those particularly of knowledge and belief, the doubts of love and sex are to be expected in a book by a young man "frightened of women." Empson, however, never seems to express fright in his amatory poems, unless "Arachne" proves the exception. The usual attitude toward sex is one of gay despair at the inevitable failure of communication, the difficulties, again, of knowing and thinking while feeling. Sometimes he is rakishly cynical in the Donne tradition. Frequently he is learnedly witty as when he proposes flight in "The World's End."

Less invitation to flee than rationalization, Empson's gay and pleasing "Invitation to Juno" shows the lover justifying his way to a presumably coy mistress. In appropriate but untraditional fashion, he suggests that they be careful of their time. Basic to this most intellectual of propositions is Ixion's seduction of Juno, but Empson also cites *De Rerum Natura* of Lucretius for authority, as well as Dr. Johnson, Othello, Darwin, and modern biological research into tissue culture. "Courage," he says, "Weren't strips of heart culture seen/ Of late mating two periodicities?" Through considerable mental agility he proves that the lovers in different cycles can come together, that the asynchronous can be made synchronous. What lady, had she the wit to follow the argument, could resist this conclusion that cohabitation is possible?

Some sort of cohabitation seems to be described in "Camping Out," which opens with the unforgettable line "And now she cleans her teeth into the lake." Empson again puts science at the service of Eros, and converts physics to poetry. The united lovers, in their bullet-boat of light, might well derange the universe with their excessive speed. The physics of quantum and space-time are used to suggest an ecstasy which makes the common world of tents and toothpaste seem unreal. Science and poetry, however, mix less successfully in "Letter IV," which proves a labored, confusing allegorization of Eddington. Often neglected by critics, there are five "letters" in *Poems* which are essentially amatory, but only tenuously related. However, it seems not an unfair generalization to say that "Letter V" may complete a circular examination of love by returning to the problem of knowledge which was the central theme of "Letter II," the first "letter" Empson published. The last of the five "letters" is in several ways the best, for Empson settles on one central analogy in "Letter V"—the locus-line-tangent-envelope analogy mentioned earlier. The resultant clarity is admirable, although hardly simple. The argument of the poem is developed logically and steadily, wit illuminating the precisely controlled conceits. In tone, imagery, and structure, therefore, "Letter V" is one of Empson's most metaphysical poems.

Two other poems in Empson's first volume of poetry, "Note on Local Flora" and "Bacchus," merit consideration. The shortest one in *Poems*, "Note on Local Flora" is also one of Empson's best remembered. The poem's brevity, polish, and deceptive simplicity, as well as its measured rhetoric, may be responsible for its popularity. Still rewarding after several readings, it continually satisfies both feeling and thought. Moreover, there are none of the excessive aridities or clotted conceits which, for many readers, mar his more ambitious poems. In contrast, "Bacchus," the longest poem, is both ambitious and clotted, although its witty complexity deserves more attention than it gets.

The local flora Empson notes is a "tree native in Turkestan" found planted in Kew Gardens. Near it is the Chinese "Tree of Heaven," botanically different from the first, but symbolically similar. The tree from Turkestan is coniferous with "hard cold cones" which "not being wards to time,/ Will leave their mother only for good cause;/ Will ripen only in a forest fire." The two in Kew, however, are similar both from their Eastern, geographical origins and from their nearly magical, mythological natures. The countries from which they come are cold, and slow to change in customs and philosophy. "One way or another," Empson has said, "the countries are supposed to fit the habits of the trees." Those people, or nations, like the tree, whose great dormant powers are utilized only in emergent occasions, are probably dull, certainly potentially destructive. Empson seems to distrust them. Shifting from botany to mythology, Empson concludes the poem with references to Semele, mother of Bacchus, and to the Phoenix which, he says, must have been a vegetable like the tree.

> So Semele desired her deity
> As this in Kew thirsts for the Red Dawn.

The poem is beautifully controlled with perfectly united analogical elements no matter how broadly or narrowly the allusions are interpreted—from the political to the personal, from the great myths of Greece, Rome, Arabia, and the Far East, to the factual account of the tree's ecology. Empson's "Local

Flora" seems to be, in Yeatsian terms, a poem "cold and passionate as the dawn."

"Bacchus," full of heat and fire, is different. At once one of Empson's longest poems, it also carries the most extensive notes. Extraordinarily complicated, it reveals the widest range of allusions and analogies of any poem. It is stylistically transitional, and is the last, most extended example of Empson's earlier metaphysical style completed at a time when he had moved to a simpler, more direct and conversational style. The first four stanzas, says Empson in his note, represent "a mythological chemical operation to distill drink." The last stanzas, five through eight, "present a person feeling tragic exultation in it." Stanza by stanza, from drink to drunkenness and the birth of Bacchus, the poem progresses in tipsy, confusing fashion. Added to the chemical, physiological, and mythical levels of the poem are teasing, historical references to Columbus, Tartar horsemen, Hitler, Mary Baker Eddy, the Japanese invasion of China, Nietzsche, and Einstein's Relativity Theory. Empson, with vaguely Joycean method, attempts to order the complexity of his poem through myth and history.

One of the predominant themes in "Bacchus," as it is in the entire volume of *Poems*, is that of man's search for a way of "maintaining oneself between contradictions." In the last stanzas of "Bacchus," Empson turns again to the death of Semele, who had been mentioned in "Local Flora." He treats her despairing questioning of her divine lover, Jupiter, her courageous daring of fate, her flaming death, and her final apotheosis. She is a sufferer who is ultimately justified, an example of human despair and the need to know. Because she attempts to bridge the gap between the extremes of heaven and earth, she is a fit representative of middling man, and, not surprisingly, she is equated with Arachne. The poem concludes with the eloquent and lyrical description of her end when, "robed in fire," she is "borne soaring forward through a crowd of cloud." In spite of the glorious, ringing finale, there are obvious weaknesses to the poem. To extend the highly allusive, densely conceited metaphysical poem to such length, to make it carry the heavy freight of so many separate themes is to overburden it. Yet if this is admitted, the poem is an impressive undertaking which is remarkably successful.

If *Poems* reflects the despair of a young man frightened of many things, as Empson told Christopher Ricks, the second book of poetry, *The Gathering Storm* (1940), "is all about politics, saying we're going to have this second world war and we mustn't get too frightened about it." While many poems in the volume do certainly express anxieties over political crises during the period from 1935 to 1940, others do not. Empson's development in style and subject matter is relative, gradual, and tentative, but there is a discernible move in the later poetry to more political themes which are communicated with greater openness and with fewer of the brain-wracking ingenuities of the metaphysical manner. He displays in his later poems the calmly despairing attitude of one private life to the noisy public events of the 1930s, the era tagged by Auden a "low dishonest decade."

Among the poems in the new manner, "Aubade" wittily combines sex, international politics, and an obviously personal experience. A dawn poem with a difference, it is based on Empson's stay in Japan in the early 1930s when, as he told Christopher Ricks, young Englishmen were warned to avoid Japanese girls because of approaching trouble between the countries. The Tokyo earthquake of 1931 awakens the lovers of Empson's poem who have obviously not taken their elders' advice. The result of the quake is seriocomic—broken bottles, scattered books, startled sleepers in a precariously balanced house on a cliff who think that, after all, it may be "the best thing to be up and go." This telling refrain is balanced by another refrain, "the heart of standing is you cannot fly," both of which are repeated alternately at the end of each stanza. Having escaped from the various economic or political disasters at home in Europe, the lover finds only quakes and pains of another kind in the Orient. To act or not to act is the question Empson poses in this poem for anyone caught in the political and social complexities of the 1930s. The poem ends with the ironic assertion of the principle that there is no other escape except submission to the inescapable.

One of Empson's most overtly political poems, "Reflections from Rochester," together with a companion poem, "Courage Means Running," presents his reflections on the critical events of 1936. The very obliqueness of these reflections, however, the indirectness of Empson's approach leading through quotations from Rochester or John Bunyan, and the dispassionate objectivity of his judgments distinguish these poems from those of Auden, Spender, or Day Lewis. Clearly about the explosive international scene—military rearmament, the "nationalist war"— "Reflections from Rochester" is also, in a larger sense, about man's compulsive actions in the face of fear. The occasion may be the Spanish Civil War, or the growing threat of German arms, but the poem seems more of a comment on human psychology, on man's desperately rationalized morality, than an antiwar tract. Furthermore, while witty, "Rochester" reveals neither didacticism nor whimsy. Serious without being solemn, the poem combines the formal elegance of terza rima with the colloquial speech rhythms Empson begins to exploit more frequently in his later poems. The quotation of the Earl of Rochester's poetry as a point of departure for Empson's poem is significant. Suggesting theme ("wretched Man is still in arms for Fear"), it also serves as an example of stylish moral indignation.

[41]

There are three quotations from *A Satire against Mankind* strategically placed in Empson's poem. These quotations are taken from the savagely satirical section where Rochester compares the predatory birds and beasts which kill from biological necessity, with depraved man who kills his fellow man from wantonness. Empson, in the first half of "Rochester," expands on the desperate compulsion and rationalization of man who has betrayed himself through fear. The second half of "Rochester" makes the theme of arms and the man more obvious than it has been. The increasing power of weaponry available to man makes self-deception no longer easy as he continues his tortured flight from fear to arms. Man now turns "blank eyes" upon his origins, the natural world of beasts "where first the race of armament was made," hoping to discern a "pattern" or explanation of his plight. "Blank" is the perfect word for the unseeing, uncomprehending look of modern man bent obsessively on self-destruction.

"Courage Means Running," written in terza rima, is stanzaically and thematically related to "Rochester." It further examines the problem of action or escape first treated in "Aubade." The note to "Courage" explains that the general "crisis-feeling" of the mid-1930s prompted the poem, the time when Germans invaded the Rhineland and the Italians conquered Ethiopia. As before, however, Empson goes far beyond particular events, which are left unidentified, to make a moralist's judgment about contemporary man. In "Courage" he uses references to Bunyan's Mr. Fearing and Much-afraid from *Pilgrim's Progress* to comment on the inextricable links between fear and courage. There can be no escape from fear, Empson decides, because courage means fear, and they both require pain. Self-respect and self-understanding, as in the case of Bunyan, come when fear is taken as the measure of man. The "flat patience" of England, or its policy of "clinging" in the face of international disaster, is, finally, about all there is "that we dare to praise."

"Ignorance of Death," a related poem, appears to continue the dialogue on life and death. Its position in *Gathering Storm* next to "Rochester" and "Courage" rounds out an examination of man's darker motives to action or inaction. Empson concludes his poem by feeling, he says, "very blank upon this topic."

The terse understatement, the flat, conversational, unmetaphoric style, and the tone of calm sanity covering strong emotions, apparent in "Ignorance of Death," are characteristic of many of the later poems. "Let It Go" is exemplary. This brief, six-line poem, added with a few others to the poems in his two previous volumes to form the first edition of the *Collected Poems* (1949), shows his final stylistic development. Deceptively simple, carefully rhymed, "Let It Go" is eloquent if not elegant. The poem is partly, and movingly, about the protective blankness and fatigue which the mind adopts to prevent madness from excessive mental and emotional experience. The more that happens to you, says Empson, the more you are unable to remember or to express verbally. "It is this deep blankness is the real thing strange." Empson, with calculated casualness, shows impressive control over the world-wide condition of "madhouse and the whole thing there."

As a poet, if not as a prose writer, Empson is a stylist. The elegance and colloquialism, the careful control of language, the exploitation of ambiguity, irony, and wit through the metaphysical conceit, the use of traditional stanzaic patterns for untraditional purposes, all identify the early Empsonian style. The later style, where it is distinguishable from the earlier, has its own characteristics, emphasizing the prosaic, unrhetorical, and conversational line, usually end-stopped, which turns on

[43]

negatives or colorless, unimportant little words ("blank," "flat") to give a strange sense of profundity. At times, among the poems appearing after "Bacchus," Empson continues in the earlier style as with "Four Legs, Three Legs, Two Legs," a densely allusive, but gay and thoroughly engaging, poem on the nature of men and sphinxes. He can also amplify the later style with lyrical innovations as in "The Teasers," inventing an original and striking verse form, resembling terza rima with half lines.

Empson advocates learning "a style from a despair" in his typically stylish "Last Pain," but he seems to recognize the dangers of mannerisms which can become obsessive or restrictive. In "Autumn on Nan-Yueh," he admits that "all styles can come down to noise." This poem, the longest of his *Collected Poems*, is appropriately in the relaxed and conversational phrases of his later style. It is also his most autobiographical poem, and, if not an unqualified critical success, it does provide a relaxed and unhurried comment on his thoughts and experiences in wartime China as he fled into exile with the Pekinese universities. Properly about flight, escapism, courage, and political involvement, it sounds the themes of many of the other poems in the volume. Stoical Empson, cheerful amidst danger and discomfort, sums things up in "Nan-Yueh" with unusual openness and ease.

Empson's clear-sighted recognition of alternatives and his acceptance, with despairing but witty grace, of "the whole thing there," make him an unusual poet of despair. He seldom resorts to satire, nor does he seek the vigorous self-help of the activists. Empson is distinguishable from the early, despairing Auden by his quiet avoidance of the more clamorous programs of social change. He also rejects the comforts of Christianity accepted by T. S. Eliot, or later by Auden, preferring the special loneliness of the atheistic rationalist who places no particular trust even in the mind. Perhaps what makes Empson's jaunty despair so impressive is the obvious strength, sanity, and balance of his mind which is able to surmount any trivial or temporary depression. Behind Empson's intelligent coping with despair is a moral integrity, a skepticism, a passionate commitment to an examination of possibilities which makes his painfully, tentatively achieved balance convincing proof of moral honesty. As in his prose, so in his poetry, Empson demands of his readers the same rigorous, yet spirited, exercise of the rational mind.

SELECTED BIBLIOGRAPHY

NOTE: *For a useful and preliminary bibliography, see Peter Low-bridge, "An Empson Bibliography," The Review, June, 1963, pp. 63–73.*

PRINCIPAL WORKS OF WILLIAM EMPSON

Seven Types of Ambiguity. London, Chatto & Windus, 1930; New York, Harcourt, Brace, 1931; 2d ed., rev., London, Chatto & Windus, 1947 (also in paperback); New York, New Directions, 1947; 3d ed., rev., London, Chatto & Windus, 1953; New York, Noonday, 1955.

Poems. London, Chatto & Windus, 1935.

Some Versions of Pastoral. London, Chatto & Windus, 1935. New ed., New York, New Directions, 1950. English Pastoral Poetry (American title of Some Versions of Pastoral). New York, Norton, 1938.

The Gathering Storm. London, Faber & Faber, 1940.

Collected Poems. New York, Harcourt, Brace, 1949; London, Chatto & Windus, 1955, 1956; New York, Harcourt, Brace, 1961 (in paperback).

"My Credo: The Verbal Analysis," *Kenyon Review*, XII (Autumn, 1950), 594–601.

The Structure of Complex Words. London, Chatto & Windus, 1951; New York, New Directions, 1951.

"Donne the Space Man," *Kenyon Review*, XIX (Summer, 1957), 337–99.

Milton's God. London, Chatto & Windus, 1961; New York, New Directions, 1962.

"Rhythm and Imagery in English Poetry," *British Journal of Aesthetics*, II (January, 1962), 36–54.

"Conversation with Christopher Ricks," *The Review*, June, 1963, pp. 26–35.

"Phoenix and the Turtle," *Essays in Criticism*, XVI (April, 1966), 147–53.

CRITICAL WORKS AND COMMENTARY

Adams, Robert. Ikon: John Milton and the Modern Critics. Ithaca, N. Y., Cornell University Press, 1955.

Alvarez, Alfred. Stewards of Excellence: Studies in Modern English and American Poets. New York, Scribners, 1958.

Brooks, Cleanth. "Empson's Criticism," *Accent*, IV (Summer, 1944), 208–16.

Danby, John. "William Empson," *Critical Quarterly*, I (Summer, 1959), 99–104.

Dodsworth, Martin. "Empson at Cambridge," *The Review*, June, 1963, pp. 3–13.

Donoghue, Denis. "Reading a Poem: Empson's 'Arachne,' " *Studies*, XLV (Summer, 1956), 219–26.

Drew, Elizabeth, and John Sweeney. Directions in Modern Poetry. New York, Norton, 1940.

Duncan, Joseph. The Revival of Metaphysical Poetry. Minneapolis, University of Minnesota Press, 1959.

Eberhart, Richard. "Empson's Poetry," *Accent*, IV (Summer, 1944), 195–207.

Falck, Colin. "This Deep Blankness," *The Review*, June, 1963, pp. 49–61.

Fraser, G. S. The Modern Writer and His World. New York, Criterion, 1955.

———. "On the Interpretation of the Difficult Poem," in Interpretations, ed. John Wain. London, Routledge and Kegan Paul, 1955.

———. Vision and Rhetoric. London, Faber & Faber, 1959.

Fuller, John. "Empson's Tone," *The Review*, June, 1963, pp. 21–25.

Hamilton, Ian. "A Girl Can't Go On Laughing All the Time," *The Review*, June, 1963, pp. 36–42.

Hedges, William. "The Empson Treatment," *Accent*, XVII (Autumn, 1957), 231–41.

Hobsbaum, Philip. "Empson as Critical Practitioner," *The Review*, June, 1963, pp. 14–20.

Hyman, Stanley Edgar. The Armed Vision. New York, Knopf, 1948.

Jensen, James. "The Construction of *Seven Types of Ambiguity*," *MLQ*, XXVII (September, 1966), 243–59.

Leavis, F. R. New Bearings in English Poetry. New York, George Stewart, 1950.

McLuhan, H. M. "Poetic vs. Rhetorical Exegesis: The Case for Leavis against Richards and Empson," *Sewanee Review*, LII (Spring, 1944), 266–76.

Morelli, Angelo. La Poesia di William Empson. Catania, Italy, Giannotta, 1959.

Olsen, Elder. "William Empson, Contemporary Criticism, and

Poetic Diction," in Critics and Criticism, ed. R. S. Crane and others. Chicago, University of Chicago Press, 1952.

Ormerod, David. "Empson's 'Invitation to Juno,'" *Explicator*, Vol. XXV (October, 1966).

Richards, I. A. "William Empson," *Furioso*, Vol. I (January 12, 1940), Supplement.

Sale, Roger. "The Achievement of William Empson," *Hudson Review*, XIX (Autumn, 1966), 369–90.

Sleight, Richard. "Mr. Empson's Complex Words," *Essays in Criticism*, II (July, 1952), 325–37.

Spector, Robert. "Form and Content in Empson's 'Missing Dates,'" *MLN*, LXXIV (April, 1959), 310–11.

Strickland, Geoffrey. "The Criticism of William Empson," *Mandrake*, II (Autumn–Winter, 1954–55), 320–31.

———. "The Poetry of William Empson," *Mandrake*, II (1953), 245–55.

Touster, Saul. "Empson's 'Legal Fiction,'" *The Review*, June, 1963, pp. 45–48.

Wain, John. Preliminary Essays. London, Macmillan, 1957.

COLUMBIA ESSAYS ON MODERN WRITERS

EDITOR: William York Tindall

ADVISORY EDITORS:
Jacques Barzun, W.T.H. Jackson, Joseph A. Mazzeo